CW00495553

The Rabbit, The Dog & The Elephant

Shireen Walton

https://www.beeresilient.co.uk/

This is for Duchess the Rabbit, who helped many children during the COVID pandemic with her kindness and compassion.

This is for Mari and Tina, my horses, who taught me about joy for twenty-four lucky years.

This is for my dogs Molly, Layla and Tashi who showed gratitude every day of their lives.

This is for all the elephants captured or free. May we all be as forgiving as Moonflower, Moonsweet and Moonlight.

This a story about a rabbit called Duchess, a dog called Layla and a baby elephant called Moonlight.

Before you go to bed and turn out your light, imagine you met a rabbit called Duchess, a dog called Layla and a baby elephant called Moonlight.

A dreamy day when you stroked Duchess in the morning, played with Layla in the afternoon and listened to Moonlight's song in the evening.

Come and meet Duchess, Layla and Moonlight.

The Rabbit

A story about kindness and compassion

Just before you go to sleep and dream, imagine you stroked a beautiful white and fluffy rabbit called Duchess.

She is very kind, soft and loves to eat carrots. Her favourite time of the day is the morning. She loves to hop and play on the green grass.

She wants to tell her story. So come and meet her.

My name is Duchess, and I am going to chat to you about being kind.

Do you know what kindness means?

Are you kind to your friends and family?

When people are unkind to me I get very nervous.

Sometimes I shake and hide from people.

I also become very quiet.

When someone is kind to me, it changes everything. I love the beautiful flowers in the garden and the soft grass under my paws.

I adore the sun in the bright blue sky.

Kindness is when people, or other animals
I know, stroke my fluffy fur and say how
wonderful I look.

Did you know that when you stroke me it
makes me happy - but also makes you happy!

It helps you to breathe better and makes you
less anxious and worried.

Can you draw something special for a friend? How about using lots of colourful pens. You could even draw me!

That would be a really kind thing to do.

I also want to talk to you about what happens when you get a bit worried.

Or when something makes you cry? Or even when you get a bit angry.

Did you know that when you put your hand over your heart and tap it slightly with your hand and say kind words to yourself, it can make you feel better?

Try it for yourself.

When I do this, I become much more aware of my surroundings.

I want to play more and I want to learn all about this wonderful world in which we live.

The Dog:

A story about joy and gratitude

You are having a wonderful day. In the morning you cuddled Duchess, the Rabbit. Because she is so kind, she wants you to play with one of her friends.

Duchess has many friends. One of her friends is a beautiful, fluffy dog called Layla, who always wags her tail with happiness.

Layla wants to tell you her story, come and meet her.

Duchess and Layla both like to play in the grass. Layla always wags her tail.

Layla is known to be happy and grateful, even when others are sad.

Hello my name is Layla. Did you know that I have so many things to be happy about everyday.

What makes you happy?

I am so grateful for having clean water in my bowl, it makes my tail wag, my coat shine and my nose wet.

I am so grateful for my daily walks with my family. I love it when it rains and I can splash in the mud.

It makes my heart beat slowly, makes me less worried, and gives me more energy.

I am so grateful for my lovely warm bed. I love cuddling my family. I show my thanks by leaving muddy paw prints everywhere!

I am grateful when I sit in front of the fire after my long walk in the forest.

I am grateful for small things, because it makes my world shine like gold.

If I could write, it would be a thank you pawprint to my family. Every day, three times a day!

Can you draw or write a letter to someone you care about?

How about your teacher? Your parents or your grandparents? Or your best friend?

Are you grateful for your warm bed like me?

Or eating lovely food?

Or seeing your favourite person smile?

Sometimes people might be unhappy, or worried or even sad.

I will still wag my tail when I see them. I know that you can't be happy all the time.

I know you can't use your paws to show your thanks, instead you can write down three good things on a piece of paper that happened to you every day.

Put this into your favourite cookie jar at the end of each day. Look at it at the end of the week and realise you really did have a good week! If you had a tail, it would wag. A lot!

It means you are joyful, happy and like being with other people. Just like me.

The Elephant

A story about forgiveness

Before you go to sleep and dream, imagine a golden land far away. A land where you are kind like Duchess, and grateful like Layla.

Just before you go to sleep and dream, you may worry that you made a few mistakes. Duchess and Layla want you to meet a beautiful baby elephant called Moonlight. She knows all about making mistakes and forgiving herself and others.

Moonlight lives with a very loving and forgiving family in a land that is golden and green.

Moonlight wants to tell you her story.

So come and meet her.

I live with my mum, Moonflower in a place so golden that it makes your heart sing.

My grandmother, Moonsweet always sings our elephant song.

Today we are crying tears as big as the thunder clouds in the sky, because Moonsweet is singing tears of sadness. We stand by her, as she lies down, and kiss her tears away.

We hear the Medicine Man softly calling our names whispered on the wind. We see a man softly calling our names. 'Moonsweet, Moonflower, Moonlight, let me help you' he says in a whispering song.

Moonflower turns to the Medicine Man, and touches his face with her large trunk. 'I am sorry' he says to my mother, as he gives Moonsweet medicine to make her better.

I can hear her heart beat slowly, as she sings our forgiveness song. This Medicine Man is not like the poachers who have hurt her. He is kind and has regret in his voice.

The Medicine Man sings to Moonsweet, and she gracefully stands up. Her trunk reaches all the way to the sun to thank the Medicine Man for his healing song.

The Medicine Man turns to me and sings, 'We are sorry Moonlight. Know that where there is a moon in this world, there will always be moonlight to dance away the shadows'.

I forgive the Medicine Man and all his people, with my whole heart. I feel happy again. I splash with joy in the sparkling lake.

Can you say sorry like the Medicine Man? Can you forgive like Moonsweet, Moonflower and Moonlight?

The science behind the stories

The stories of Duchess, Layla and Moonlight are based on the science of positive psychology, which looks to study 'human functioning (that) aims to discover and promote the factors that allow individuals and communities to thrive." (Seligman)

Interaction with animals have shown to decrease stress, lower blood pressure and reduce loneliness. There is a growing body of research that suggests animals, especially pets, have a positive effect on your health and wellbeing, by providing a sense of purpose, social connection and reducing isolation. There is also evidence that close engagement with animals reduces panic attacks and the need to self-harm.

The effect of stress is much discussed and is seen as a major disrupter to health and wellbeing. Stress can be good. It keeps us alert and gives you the ability to respond to danger when you need to run from 'the tiger.' The stress hormone, cortisol, is released by the adrenal glands to deal with threat to help you survive. It is therefore a good thing for survival. That bit keeps you alive. Ideally, you need to come out of this stress response of flight, fight, or freeze. You need to move back to homeostasis, or a balanced state of being when the threat has gone. Animals are good at coming out of this state, by utilising their body to shake it out; to somatically move through the threat and subsequent stress response, they return to a happy state of being, especially when they live in their natural environment. You are supposed to do the same, but you could stay continuously in the stress response, making you anxious and wreaking havoc with your immune system. Environmental, genetic or food factors may also contribute to keeping your stress response activated.

You are also predisposed to focus on the negative because you are wired to danger which stops you, metaphorically, from being eaten by the tiger. Getting stuck on the negative, especially if it's trauma induced keeps the cortisol running in your system. It is working overtime and can be physically exhausting. Positive psychology offers interventions to break the activated stress response, by improving the development of your neural pathways in your brain. These pathways can become stilted or frayed under stress, which can inhibit the development of character strengths, which are the building blocks for happiness and wellbeing.

This book uses storytelling to combine your relationship with animals with three positive psychology character strengths: Loving kindness, Gratitude and Forgiveness. Introducing these character strengths into your daily life provides the building blocks for resilience and happiness.

Working with Loving Kindness, Gratitude and Forgiveness as character strengths helps you to physically build the wiring in your brain. Development of this wiring works on your neurotransmitters, responsible for managing information about your emotional state around your body. Re-wiring your emotional state can happen at any age. It's called neuroplasticity, so it's never too late.

Duchess, the rabbit, encourages us all to practice Loving- Kindness no matter how old we are.

The visualisation of hugging yourself or touching a furry pet, like a rabbit, helps you to develop close connection with your feelings. The metaphor of Duchess becomes a safe way to engage those feelings of connection. Stroking an animal or tapping on your heart with your hands, has been shown to reduce stress, by activating the happy hormone oxytocin, thereby reducing stress in your body. It provides a calming effect on the body, helping us to feel safe. Feeling safe makes us feel less anxious.

Layla, the dog, demonstrates the character strength of Gratitude. The simple act of being thankful, daily for the small things in life will have a really positive effect on you. Research shows that gratitude, or giving thanks, is one of the key strengths that contributes to our happiness and wellbeing. Becoming aware that good things can happen, even if life is presenting us with the negative, gives us the tools to rebalance your wellbeing. In the story, Layla is grateful for the small things in life. She is grateful for a bowl of clean water and shows it by wagging her tail.

Moonlight, the elephant, celebrates the act of Forgiveness as a character strength with her elephant family, Moonsweet and Moonflower. As a metaphor, the elephants are forgiving. Forgiveness accepts the shortcoming of others, gives second chances, avoids vengeance. It's about letting go of hurt when wronged. It is one of the most challenging of character strengths, because suffering caused by others, can be all consuming. Forgiveness is not about denial, condoning pardoning or forgetting a wronged act. It takes work, it takes time. The benefits of practising forgiveness associates with physical and psychological health. You may find yourself being less angry, anxious, or depressed. When you forgive someone totally, you will feel the physical effects in your body. Practising this in combination with Loving Kindness and Gratitude contribute to a forgiveness process that will require repetition over an unlimited period.

The practice of these character strengths, supported by the kindness of animals, helps us to be resilient. This knowledge will give you the fortitude to tackle the difficult times in your life and the wisdom to celebrate the good that life has to offer.

Workbook- Exercises to help build your resilience.

We know that practice really helps. Think of it as developing a new muscle; you need to exercise it to see the results. Below are several exercises or interventions that you can practice as a family, group of friends, or with your favourite animal.

Loving Kindness Exercise 1 - Body Scan and Mindfulness (Based on the work by Kristin Neff)

The purpose of this exercise is to become fully mindful of one's own body, and to engage the parasympathetic nervous system and release the happy hormone, oxytocin. Sometimes, through stress or a traumatic event, you can disengage emotionally from your own body, and that can stop you from being fully present to what is good for you. Sometimes this connection can be difficult, so we always ask Duchess to help us with this. Research has shown that a looking at a picture can really help with this.

Body Scan with Duchess

- Focus on her ears and breathe deeply, and ask her what she is hearing.
- Focus on her eyes and breathe deeply, and ask her what her might be seeing.
- Focus on the nose and breathe deeply, and ask her what she might be smelling.
- Focus on the mouth and breathe deeply, and ask her what she might be tasting.
- Focus on her neck and shoulders, and ask her if she has is comfortable or has any pain.

- Focus on her heart and breathe deeply, gently stroke her heart, and tell her that you love her.
- Focus on her tummy and breathe very deeply, and ask her if she is comfortable or has any pain.
- Focus on her hips, breathe, very deeply, and ask her if she is comfortable or has any pain.
- Focus on her back, and breathe very deeply and ask her if she is comfortable or has any pain.
- Focus on her legs and toes, and breathe very deeply, and ask her if she comfortable or has any pain.
- You can spend as long or as little on this exercise. A minute a day will do, but the more often and longer you do it the more fun and beneficial it will be.
- When you are ready, you can try doing a body scan on yourself:
- Focus on your ears and breathe deeply, and ask what you can hear.
- Focus on your eyes and breathe deeply, and ask what you can see.
- Focus on your nose and breathe deeply, and ask what you can smell.
- Focus on your mouth and breathe deeply, and ask you what you can taste.
- Focus on your neck and shoulders, and ask if you are comfortable or have any pain.
- Focus on your heart and breathe deeply, gently stroke your heart, and say that you love you.
- Focus on your tummy and breathe very deeply, and ask if you are comfortable or have any pain.
- Focus on your hips, breathe, very deeply, and ask if you are comfortable or have any pain.
- Focus on your back and breathe very deeply and ask if you are comfortable or have any pain.

- Focus on your legs and toes, and breathe very deeply, and ask if you are comfortable or have any pain.

Loving Kindness Exercise 2- Heart to Heart exercises (Based on the work by Kristin Neff)

- Duchess loves to be stroked. It de-activates the sympathetic nervous system, helping Duchess to calm down and feel safe. She loves it, and we know through scientific research that physical touch helps to release oxytocin, which can take away emotions that upset us and calms down the cardiovascular system, lowering blood pressure. It's basically good for all of us!
- You can do this as often as you like.
- Visualise stroking Duchess over her body and particularly her heart area or stroke your own pet at home.
- Then place both your hands over your heart, and gently stroke the heart area, sometimes in round circles. You can also touch your cheek if you feel more comfortable or rub your tummy.

This is a way to show kindness and compassion to yourself and other animals. Remember if you touch animals do it either under professional observation, or if it's your own pet, always check that it's safe to do so. And like Duchess, be careful of strangers.

Gratitude Exercise 3- Joy and Gratitude

The power of Gratitude is probably one of the most researched interventions in Positive Psychology. According to Robert Emmons, an eminent psychologist, it has the power to heal, energise and change lives.

Grateful people identify good things in their life, recognise the source or cause of goodness, and are consequently more socially engaged, satisfied and happier with life.

Living life with gratitude is part of everyday life. Layla for example, lives a grateful life. She accepts both good and bad, always remaining grateful for the small things in her life. She sees life as a gift. She is joyous and grateful, giving her an attitude to manage grief and anxiety.

A - The Gratitude List: Based on the work of Martin Seligman

Layla is very aware of what she is grateful for on a day to day basis. She is happy with clean water and tasty food. You can make a list of what you are grateful for and place it on the fridge for example. It can be a list of people who helped you that day, or being grateful for your pet. Sharing it with your friends and family helps to build the gratitude practice and allow those neurotransmitters to do their work.

B- A Gratitude Letter

Writing a gratitude letter is something that you could share with someone that has had an impact on your life, both good and bad. You may not want to send it, but it helps to you reflect on the experience and see how it has brought you to this moment in time.

C- The Cookie Jar

Dog lovers and owners all know that dogs can leap with joy when you open the Jar of Gratitude, and give them a titbit or a treat. They may have been naughty, chewed your favourite book and spent time in the dog house, but everything is soon forgotten when the cookie jar is open and shared. If we keep a jar and write three good things that have happened to us in that day, no matter what might have happened, it helps us to recognise those moments of joy and assists us to come through periods of grief, giving us the strength to look beyond it. It makes us resilient and stronger. You could reflect on the contents of the cookie jar at the end of the week, or month. Or some people do it at the end of the year.

Exercise 4- Forgiveness (Based on the work of Witvliet et al)

Moonlight's elephant family were quick to forgive the Medicine Man all human transgressions and mistakes and recognised that he was there to help. All animals do have long memories though, especially elephants. They grieve, cry, and suffer immense trauma, mostly at the hand of humans. It is a wishful thought, that elephants can forgive us our transgressions, as Moonlight's family did so easily. I hope that we can find a way to heal the rift that sits between us and the animal kingdom. We need to create balance and homeostasis with our relationship with the animals. Forgiveness may be a way to heal this rift, however difficult, so that we can move beyond anger and anxiety, to harmony and happiness.

This exercise asks you to understand why the person has been offensive? This can generate compassion and see the offender as not all bad or all good. Understanding why a bully behaves as they do can help to understand they they may have a story too. It is not to give permission for their behaviour, condone it, or forget it. Can we forgive the elephant poacher, understand that he needs to provide for his family? Can we reprimand appropriately and provide a solution that stops this offender from re offending? These are tough questions, and it takes time to process.

My thoughts

I hope that the stories have served to help you all on your journey to wellness and happiness. So far, the research shows it works, and from my experience working with clients I have seen remarkable results.

Shireen Walton

Beeresilient.co.uk

Bibliography

The science of positive psychology is constantly adding to its body of knowledge thanks to the academics and researchers in this field. The following is an example of the research we have used in the stories. This is an exciting field, and we urge you to investigate for yourself. At Beeresilient, we have found that having knowledge, understanding the why, has helped our clients to heal and become resilient for life.

Canine Charter for Human Health (2008). Retrieved from http://www.dogstrust.org.uk/press_office/pressreleases/2008/caninecharter.htm

Crowley-Robinson, P., Fenwick, D.C. & Blackshaw, J.K. (1996) A long-term study of elderly people in nursing homes with visiting and resident dogs. *Applied Animal Behaviour Science, 47, (1-2)* 137-148

Csikszentmihalyi, M. (1990). Flow: The psychology of optimal experience. Harper& Row

Emmons, R. A., & McCullough, M. E. (2004). *The Psychology of Gratitude (Series in Affective Science).* New York: Oxford University Press.

Ekman, P., & Davidson, R. J. (1993). Voluntary smiling changes regional brain activity. *Psychological Science, 4*(5), 342-345.

Gordon, A. M., Impett, E. A., Kogan, A., Oveis, C., & Keltner, D. (2012). To have and to hold: Gratitude promotes relationship maintenance in intimate bonds. *Journal of personality and social psychology, 103*(2), 257.

Hawkins, R. D., Hawkins, E. L., & Tip, L. (2021). "I can't give up when I have them to care for": People's experiences of pets and their mental health. Anthrozoös, 34(4), 543–562.

https://doi.org/10.1080/08927936.2021.1914434

Hayden-Evans, M., Milbourn, B., & Netto, J. (2018). 'Pets provide meaning and purpose': A
qualitative study of pet ownership from the perspectives of people diagnosed with borderline personality disorder. Advances in Mental Health, 16(2), 152–162.
https://doi.org/10.1080/18387357.2018.1485508

Jarden, A., Rashid, T., Roache, A., & Lomas, T. (2019). Ethical guidelines for positive psychology practice (version 1.0: English). International Journal of Wellbeing, 9(3), 1–30.
https://doi.org/10.5502/ijw.v9i3.921

Jones, M. G., Rice, S. M., & Cotton, S. M. (2019). Incorporating animal-assisted therapy in mental health treatments for adolescents: A systematic review of canine assisted psychotherapy.

Lau, R. W., & Cheng, S. T. (2011). Gratitude lessens death anxiety. *European Journal of Ageing, 8*(3), 169.

Luhmann, M., & Kalitzki, A. (2018). How animals contribute to subjective well-being: A comprehensive model of protective and risk factors. Journal of Positive Psychology, 13(2),
200–214. https://doi.org/10.1080/17439760.2016.1257054

Korb, A. (2012). *The Grateful Brain.* Retrieved from https://www.psychologytoday.com/au/blog/prefrontal-nudity/201211/the-grateful-brain

McGrath, R. E. (2015). Character strengths in 75 nations: An update. Journal of Positive Psychology, 10, 41–52.
https://doi.org/10.1080/17439760.2014.888580

Neff, K. D. & Germer, C. (2017). Self-Compassion and Psychological Wellbeing. In J. Doty (Ed.) Oxford Handbook of Compassion Science, Ch. 27. Oxford University Press.

Kristine Neff : https://self-compassion.org/

Niemiec, R. M. (2018). Character strengths interventions: A field-guide for practitioners. Hogrefe.

Niemiec, R. M. (2019). A simple model for working with strengths. VIA Institute on Character. https://www.viacharacter.org/topics/articles/a-simple-model-for-working-with-strength

Peterson, C., & Seligman, M. P. (2004). Character strengths and virtues: A handbook and
classification. Oxford University Press.

Phelps, K. A, Miltenberger, R.G, Jens, T & Wadeson, H (2008). An investigation of the effects of dog visits on depression, mood, and social interaction in elderly individuals- living in a nursing home. *Behavioral Interventions, 23(3)*, 181-200.

Salzberg, S. (2013). Real happiness at work: meditations for accomplishment, achievement, and peace. New York: Workman Publishing Company, Inc. https://www.sharonsalzberg.com/

Schroeder, K., Stroud, D., Sherwood, D. M., & Udell, M. A. (2018). Therapeutic factors in equine-facilitated group psychotherapy for women survivors of interpersonal violence. Journal for Specialists in Group Work, 43(4), 326–348. https://doi.org/10.1080/01933922.2018.1516707

Schroeder, Katy & Prasath, Priscilla. (2022). Positive Psychology and Therapy Animals: A Conceptual Integration for Counseling Practice. Journal of Mental Health Counselling. 44. 312-326. 10.17744/mehc.44.4.03.

Seligman, M. E. (2011). Flourish: A visionary new understanding of happiness and well-being. Simon and Schuster

Serpell, J. (1990) Evidence for long term effects of pet ownership on human health In Pets, *Benefits and Practice Waltham Symposium 20,* April 19 1990

Ma, L. K., Tunney, R. J., & Ferguson, E. (2017). Does gratitude enhance prosociality? A meta-analytic review. *Psychological Bulletin, 143*(6), 601–635. http://dx.doi.org/10.1037/bul0000103

Nagasawa, M. et al. (2009). "Dog's Gaze at Its Owner Increases Owner's Urinary Oxytocin During Social Interaction," Hormones and Behavior (forthcoming). Retrieved from: http://www.newscientist.com/article/dn16412-pet-dogs-rival-humans-for-emotional-satisfaction.html

Washington State University. "Stress reduction benefits from petting dogs, cats." ScienceDaily. ScienceDaily, 15 July 2019. <www.sciencedaily.com/releases/2019/07/190715114302.htm>.

vanOyen Witvliet C, Ludwig TE, Vander Laan KL. Granting forgiveness or harboring grudges: implications for emotion, physiology, and health. Psychol Sci. 2001 Mar;12(2):117-23. doi: 10.1111/1467-9280.00320. PMID: 11340919.

Wong, Y. J., Owen, J., Gabana, N. T., Brown, J. W., McInnis, S., Toth, P., & Gilman, L. (2018). Does gratitude writing improve the mental health of psychotherapy clients? Evidence from a randomized controlled trial. *Psychotherapy Research, 28*(2), 192-202.

About the Author

Shireen Walton is a positive psychologist, IT consultant and PhD researcher into human behaviour and cyber security.

She holds a degree in History, Politics and International Relations, a post graduate certificate in Education, two Masters of Science degrees in Information Technology and Positive Psychology Coaching.

She runs a coaching practice from her home in the Cotswolds, working with all ages to improve resilience and wellbeing. She loves to ride her horses and walk her dogs in her spare time.

This is her first book.

Acknowledgements

I would like to thank all the academics and researchers who have dedicated their lives to improving and understanding the human and animal condition. I would also like to thank Lee Bown, at Belo creative for the design, Dr Steve Green for the formatting and Dr Peter Cochrane for his wisdom. I would like to thank the McMath family, especially Eve, for their continued support on this project. Suzy Dymond-White for the editing and Stephanie Jean Weager for inspiration. Nicky Amor for her equine therapy knowledge. Abby Blackwell for looking after my horses. Lorraine Hocking who made these stories possible. Finally, as always, Jamie and Andrew for putting up with my work. Molly, Tashi, Layla, Jamara, Tina, Mr Dash, Leni, Kalani, Poppy, Bambi, Fleur and Lulu for their animal happiness and resilience.

Printed in Great Britain
by Amazon

31150376R00034